Feline Groovy

Printed by St Austell Printing Company on paper produced from sustainably managed forests using vegetable-based inks.

Many thanks to Luke Murray, Lowenna Trewenna, Robert Fox, and to all friends and family for their encouragement and support.

All of my love to Karen for 'being' there. x

ISBN 978-1-5272-4546-4

British Library Cataloguing in Publication Data.
A catalogue record for this book is available from the British Library.

Tuesday Afternoon,
Daydreaming...

On Days Like These...

Blowing in the Wind

California
Dreaming

Can't Stop the Feeling

Heaven

Must

be

Missing

an

Angel

Once in a Lifetime

I'm
a
Believer

You're the One That I Want

Beautiful
Stranger

Blinded by the Light

Kiss

Watermelon Sugar

Bliss

Sunshine of Your Love

You do Something to Me

Feeling Groovy

Beautiful
Day

To Dream of Love

A Sky of Honey

Waterloo Sunset

Stay
With
Me
Promises

I
Put
a
Spell
on
You

Mr
Blue
Sky

VOUS

Let's

Dance

Night Fever

Shake
it
Off

Light
My
Fire

Higher

and

Higher

Into the Mystic

I

Feel

Love

Whole Lotta Love

London Calling

LONDON

New
York

Breakfast
in
America

I
Heard
it
Through
the
Grapevine

Wish

You

Were

Here

Don't Go Breaking My Heart

Where

is

the

Love

Miss

You

Sweet Dreams

Call
Me

GHI
DEF
ABC
1
JKL
MN
PRS
TUV
WXY
OQ
EMERGENCY CALLS
FOR
FIRE
POLICE
AMBULANCE
DIAL
999
PLEASE
59539

One
of
These
Nights

Hush

I
Promised
You
a
Miracle

Feel

You've

Got

the

Love

Say a Little Prayer

Enjoy

the

Silence

Wake
Up

A Kind of Magic

I
Can't
Explain

Faith

Let Your Love Flow

It's
a
Beautiful
World

Let

it

Be

...God Only Knows

1 *On Days Like These...*

2 Blowing in the Wind

starring **Amanda and Leah**

3 California Dreaming

starring **Ella**

4 Can't Stop the Feeling

starring **Fee**

5 Heaven Must be Missing an Angel

starring **Sparo**

6 Once in a Lifetime

starring **Amber**

7 I'm a Believer

starring **Pussycat and Juan**

8 You're the One That I Want

starring **Esmée and Sugar**

9 Beautiful Stranger

starring **Peanut**

10 Blinded by the Light

starring **Sparkle**

11 Kiss

starring **Poppy**

12 Watermelon Sugar

starring **Woody and Lily**

13 Bliss

starring **Lola**

14 Sunshine of Your Love

starring **Pisces**

15 You do Something to Me

starring
Tom

16 Feeling Groovy

starring
Duke

17 Beautiful Day

starring
Maisey

18 To Dream of Love

starring
Pisces

19 A Sky of Honey

starring
Cleo

20 Waterloo Sunset

starring
Jody and Eve

21 Stay With Me

starring
Madelaine

22 I Put a Spell on You

starring
Kizzy

23 Mr Blue Sky

starring
Fin

24 Let's Dance

starring
Marky, Ollie, Ells and Domy

25 Night Fever

starring
Cassius, Max, Lucas, Pablo and Milky

26 Shake it Off

starring
Rosa

27 Light My Fire

starring
Abbey and Pisces

28 Higher and Higher

starring
Bruce and Mr Whiskerton

29 Into the Mystic

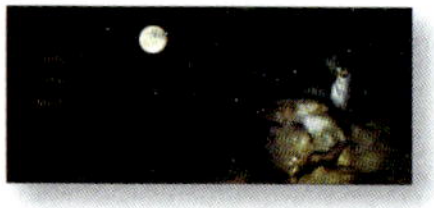

starring **Katie**

30 I Feel Love

starring **Debs**

31 Whole Lotta Love

starring **Benny**

32 London Calling

starring **Harley**

33 New York

starring **Georgina**

34 Breakfast in America

starring **Jense**

35 I Heard it Through the Grapevine

starring **Neezy and Sandy**

36 Wish You Were Here

starring **Pebbles**

37 Don't Go Breaking My Heart

starring **Pinks and Tinks**

38 Where is the Love

starring **Ziggy and Bear**

39 Miss You

starring **J**

40 Sweet Dreams

starring **Sophie**

41 Call Me

starring **Dot**

42 One of These Nights

starring **Chloe**

43 Hush

starring
Mungo, Mary, Midge and Mr Benn

44 I Promised You a Miracle

starring
Sabre and Isaac

45 Feel

starring
May

46 You've Got the Love

starring
Thea and Darling

47 Say a Little Prayer

starring
Grace

48 Enjoy the Silence

starring
Morris

49 Wake Up

starring
Pisces

50 A Kind of Magic

starring
The Amazing Faroo

51 I Can't Explain

starring
Emily

52 Faith

starring
Elise

53 Let Your Love Flow

starring
Jess

54 It's a Beautiful World

starring
Riley

55 Let it Be

starring
Alice

56 *...God Only Knows*

starring
Dudley

"That's Life!"